# WHEN LIFE MAKES
# YOU NERVOUS

*New and Effective Treatment for Anxiety*

Dr. David B. Hawkins, ACSW, Ph.D.

"Worry does not empty
tomorrow of sorrow—
it empties today of
strength."

— CORRIE TEN BOOM

"Don't worry about
the world coming to an
end today. It's already
tomorrow in Australia."

—CHARLES M. SCHULZ

Victor is an imprint of
Cook Communications Ministries, Colorado Springs, Colorado 80918
Cook Communications, Paris, Ontario
Kingsway Communications, Eastbourne, England

WHEN LIFE MAKES YOU NERVOUS
© 2001 by David B. Hawkins

ISBN: 0-78143-736-9
First Printing, 2001
Printed in the United States of America

Editors: Craig Bubeck, John Conaway
Cover & Interior Design: Global Images and iDesignEtc.

# ABOUT THE AUTHOR

A licensed clinical psychologist trained in the fields of social work and clinical psychology, Dr. David B. Hawkins, ACSW, Ph.D., has been in private practice for more than twenty years and specializes in domestic violence, adult and family issues, and marriage enrichment. Based in Longview, Washington, he is a certified domestic violence perpetrator treatment provider, certified forensic examiner, and a spiritual director. He also is a member of the National Association of Social Workers, Academy of Forensic Examiners, and the American Psychological Association. The author of several other books, including *See Dick and Jane Grow Up* (ISBN: 0-78143-498-X), David has co-hosted a weekly radio broadcast entitled "Right Where You Live," was the host of an award-winning television program entitled "Community Forum," and writes a monthly column for the *Longview Daily News* entitled "Matters of the Heart."

# INTRODUCTION

Perhaps there is no more unsettling feeling in the world than anxiety. It can grip you so fiercely that you believe you will come apart at the seams. Feeling alone in the midst of this nerve-wracking world only serves to intensify this horrific experience. Anxiety has long been the cornerstone for research into the mental arena, because to understand why we experience anxiety and how we can deal with it is to understand mental health.

The great theologian and philosopher Søren Kierkegaard said the following about anxiety: "I would say that learning to know anxiety is an adventure which every man has to affront if he would not go to perdition either by having known anxiety or by sinking under it. He, therefore, who has learned rightly to be anxious has learned the most important thing" (*The Concept of Dread*).

*This philosopher's words do not make me feel any easier about this topic. Are most of us destined to struggle with anxiety at one time or another? Certainly the answer, as we all know, is yes. Whether it is the vague feeling of dread associated with **generalized anxiety disorder**, the jitters of being in a crowd associated with **social anxiety**, or the heart palpitations associated with **panic anxiety**, all are terribly uncomfortable and, to some degree, familiar. Perhaps you come to this time in your life having struggled with challeng-*

*ing symptoms of **obsessive compulsive disorder**. Whatever your experience with anxiety, I suspect that you are eager to find answers to help allay these fears.*

Fortunately, the days of having to suffer from any of these debilitating disorders is over. **Your Pocket Therapist** is here to help you in recognizing your particular problem and assist you in finding the appropriate solution. And, if you are a newcomer to the search for answers, your search is over. Not that there are any miracle cures, but there are *real answers.*

The fact that you have picked up **Your Pocket Therapist** indicates that you are searching for some answers. Perhaps you have struggled for years only to be pacified with some condescending response like "It's all in your head, so get over it." Or some well-meaning friend or spouse has said sincerely, "I can't understand what you are feeling. What do you want me to do?" Of course, all you wanted them to do was take away this awful feeling. And, of course, they did not have the power to do that.

While sufferers of anxiety disorders feel alone and misunderstood, it is a very common problem. These problems, in fact, have been considered the most common of emotional disorders. Approximately twenty million Americans—one in nine—are affected by this problem. So it is not an uncommon problem, and there are solutions to it.

In this book, we will explore the latest that science has to offer us on these very treatable conditions. Let's get started.

# HISTORICAL PERSPECTIVE

Sadly, we do not hear many people talking about their struggles with anxiety disorders. This is one category of mental health problems that seems to have been tagged with extra baggage so that it is not safe to talk about. We are finally getting to the point where we can talk about depression and not feel like second-class citizens. We can even admit that we have gone to therapy. Marriage problems can be admitted and even discussed openly. Why, then, I wonder, can we not admit that we struggle with anxiety?

I do not know the answer to that question. I only know that it is well beyond time that we bring this disorder out in the open and share the wealth of information available to all who desperately need it.

There was a time when we thought the way to deal with anxiety was to "grin and bear it." Another solution was long-term therapy to discover the hidden roots to the problem that lay buried deep within the psyche of the sufferer. In other words, you had to be very wealthy and patient to gain any relief from anxiety. But now that we have done research on particular therapy methods, we find that those long-term methods were no more effective—perhaps even less so—than the short-term, solution-focused therapies that are emerging today.

The old premise was that there was some dark, hidden conflict that needed to be exposed to the light. Therefore, the theory posited, reminiscing and emoting about childhood events would be good for the "patient." For some it may be helpful to talk about their childhood memories, but for others it is largely ineffective in healing their symptoms. Now we know that a messed-up childhood may or may not be associated with symptoms of anxiety. Those with troubled pasts may have anxiety disorders, but so might those with relatively healthy upbringings.

We know much more today than we did ten, twenty, or thirty years ago. So what have the last twenty years taught us? Let's take a look.

# TYPES OF ANXIETY DISORDERS

For starters we now know that there is more than one kind of anxiety disorder, and different approaches and medications are effective with each one. So we dare not clump all anxious people into one category. Let's briefly look at each disorder; then we will set out the solutions and therapies appropriate for each one. We will also look at an individual who has struggled with an anxiety disorder and what efforts have been made at resolving her problem.

# GENERAL SYMPTOMS OF ANXIETY

Now that we have laid out some of the general categories of anxiety, let's take a look at the typical symptoms we're referring to when we use the word *anxiety*. While anxiety can mean different things to different people, most psychologists would agree that the following symptoms apply to this disorder:

- Worry or fear that something bad will happen
- Nervousness
- Muscle tension or jitteriness
- Heart palpitations
- Dry mouth, nausea
- Sweating and cold, clammy hands
- Fatigue or restlessness
- Uncontrollable obsessive thoughts
- Painful, intrusive memories

The particular anxiety disorders are usually categorized as follows:

**Generalized Anxiety Disorder (GAD).** People who experience GAD typically have worries that interfere with their daily functioning. They may constantly worry about several issues that they cannot dismiss. Their concerns may be about money, sex, family, or work. The important thing in this disorder is that it interferes with people's ability to concentrate and makes them irritable and exhausted. This particular disorder is sometimes associated with other mental health problems such as depression or substance abuse.

**Phobias.** These are unrealistic fears about certain objects or situations. It is an unrealistic, persistent fear of a specific object. The fear is often so great that the person will go to great lengths to avoid contact with the feared object. For example, agoraphobia, or the fear of open places, is quite common today. Many are unfortunately held captive in their homes because of their fear of going outdoors.

Another common type of phobia is social phobia. This has been described as "an intense fear of becoming humiliated in social situations, specifically embarrassing yourself in front of other people" (National Institute of Mental Health). These individuals fear that all of the focus is on them and that people will notice their tiniest mistakes. They perceive themselves as being inept, and others as being much more socially capable.

A young man writes, "I did not want to go to parties. I would feel really self-conscious and could only feel OK if I had some beers in me. Then I would feel better. Otherwise I would fear that everyone was looking at me and would make fun of me if I did something wrong. I would rather not go to these parties, but didn't want to sit in my room while others were out having fun."

**Panic Anxiety.** This is an intense fear with accompanying feelings of panic such as heart palpitations, nausea, and shortness of breath. It can occur for no apparent reason, making it all the more disconcerting.

Listen as a young man describes his experience: "It started about ten years ago when I was sitting in a seminar. The room was warm and humid. The room was not well ventilated, and I felt uncomfortable. I was tired from working hard that week. The panic attack was a violent experience for me. I felt like I was going insane. My heart started pounding rapidly, the room felt like it was closing in around me, and I felt slightly disoriented. I had a strong feeling of impending doom. As if that experience was not bad enough, I now fear that I will have that experience again, which sometimes brings on another attack."

**Obsessive Compulsive Disorder (OCD).** OCD is characterized by repeated, unwanted thoughts or compulsive behaviors. There may be irrational thoughts that the person is unable to dismiss. Attempts to use common-sense reasoning are, unfortunately, unsuccessful in dispelling these thoughts. Individuals often attempt to get rid of unwanted thoughts by using repetitive rituals, or compulsions, to reduce their anxiety. For example, an obsessions involving dirt or germs can lead to compulsive behaviors of hand-washing or cleaning.

Let's listen to someone who struggles with OCD: "I had a ritual for everything. It began with counting things. I had to count the number of times I washed my hands before and after a meal. I couldn't touch anything that I thought had gotten dirty. Dirt was almost evil to me. Even though I knew it was irrational, I feared that if I touched something dirty I would catch some horrible disease. So, I keep myself perfectly clean and wash my clothes at least twice a day. I also shower at least twice a day. It is exhausting."

**Posttraumatic Stress Disorder (PTSD).** PTSD occurs when someone has experienced something that is out of the realm of normal experience and with which they are not prepared to cope. This diagnosis first appeared with veterans of combat, but the syndrome is now recognized to exist within others who have experienced severe trauma.

Individuals with PTSD have experienced a severe emotional or physical event, such as an industrial accident, sexual assault, or natural disaster such as a fire. Memories of the event continue to flood the individual through nightmares, intrusive thoughts, or flashbacks. They may also feel numb, jittery, or depressed when thinking about the particular trauma. They often feel detached, on guard, and have trouble sleeping.

A woman responds to questions about her PTSD: "I was molested by my uncle when I was ten. It happened several times in spite of my efforts to make him stop. I was afraid to tell my parents because they might not believe me. After all, he was my

"WHO OF YOU BY WORRYING CAN ADD A SINGLE HOUR TO HIS LIFE?"

—*Matthew 6:27*

mom's brother. Well, now I have flashbacks about the experience. I can't have normal sexual relations without thinking about this man touching me. When I see someone who looks like him, all the bad feelings come flooding back."

## TAMMY'S STORY

Let's peek into the life of one woman who has struggled with anxiety for many years, only to remain frustrated and discouraged that she will ever find a remedy to her problem. Tammy, with her husband Rick, had come in for marriage counseling a few months ago due to increased conflict in their relationship.

Tammy is a twenty-eight-year-old mother of two children, married to Rick for six years, and employed as a schoolteacher. Already you may be saying to yourself, "Yikes! She has her hands full!" Indeed she does, and she is feeling some symptoms of anxiety.

She began developing her symptoms gradually. It was not like she woke up one morning and all of a sudden felt that her world was out of control. She began to notice her hyperarousal, startle reflex, and jitteriness. She attributed her emerging symptoms to "stress" and vowed to cut back on some of her obligations. However, being a perfectionist by nature, this was not always easy to do.

Tammy, as you might imagine, was trying to juggle many things in her life. As a teacher of third graders she wanted to do her best. She had only been a teacher for five years and was still trying to make a positive impression. Besides, she mused, she really enjoyed her kids and teaching. For any of you familiar with the teaching profession, a teacher's day does not end when the kids leave at 3:30. Tammy would usually take work home and try to juggle work assignments with feeding her two young children, cleaning the home, and preparing for the next day's challenges.

Rick was a supportive husband. As a construction worker, his hours were a little more unpredictable, but he was willing to help. He watched her begin to unravel, slowly but surely. Rick shares his thoughts with us: "I watched her coming home night after night and staying up until eleven grading papers and then getting up at the crack of dawn to exercise, feed the kids, and get to school. It has been frustrating to see her become more irritable, depressed, and edgy. The slightest thing seems to set her off. We are even bickering more than ever. I sometimes wonder about our decision to have kids and both work. It feels like too much."

Tammy shares her perspective on the situation: "I have always wanted to be a teacher, and there is no good time to have kids. I thought that I should have them while we are young and have the energy to enjoy them. I cannot see myself cutting corners on my work at school. The principal and other teachers expect a certain level of performance, and I am not going to let them down. As for exercising and singing in the choir, those things are for me. But I have to admit that I am becoming more tired, irritable, and discouraged."

As this couple sat with me discussing their marriage problems, it was clear that there were several layers to their problem. Not only did they need to do some work on their relationship—specifically, communication skills and methods of developing intimacy—but it appeared that Tammy had developed an anxiety disorder as well.

During one session we spent considerable time exploring her symptoms and feelings. She tearfully shared that she was not sleeping well, felt uptight and edgy much of the time, had nausea at times, and occasionally had what sounded like panic attacks. She would suddenly develop shortness of breath, jitteriness, and heart palpitations. Her doctor had examined her on one occasion, but was unable to give a medical explanation. This is partially what led them to my office.

During this visit we decided that since her physician had examined her and found no medical causes for her symptoms, and because her lifestyle was so stress-provoking, we decided that this was the place to begin. However, Tammy was counseled, making changes in one's temperament and lifestyle are never as easy as they sound. Few of us really want to make significant changes in our lives. Rather, crises happen that cause us to reexamine our values and how we are living our lives.

Over the course of the next several months we worked together to look at the familial predisposition to her anxiety, the obvious lifestyle issues, and possible biochemical implications as well. The causes of her anxiety, as for most sufferers of anxiety disorders, were many. A variety of approaches would prove successful at alleviating the majority of her painful symptoms.

# CAUSES OF ANXIETY

It is, sadly, common for individuals with anxiety disorders to feel like they are failures. They tend to feel a sense of shame and inadequacy that they cannot control their feelings or thoughts. Typically perfectionists, this lack of control only adds to their feelings of inferiority. They also often perceive others as having greater coping abilities. As I said, we have kept the topic of anxiety disorders in the closet for so long that those with this problem feel isolated and alone.

But why is anxiety such a common phenomenon, and what are the causes? This is a difficult and complex question, and new answers are being discovered every day.

While there is much that we do not know, we are learning more all the time. For example, we know that anxiety runs in families, leading us to speculate that there is a strong genetic predisposition toward this disorder. Researchers have found that if one identical twin has an anxiety disorder, it is likely that the other will have one as well.

In addition to genetics, it would appear that life experiences also play a role in this disorder. Obviously those who experience unstable backgrounds will likely have more anxiety than those whose upbringing was stable and predictable. Likewise, someone who has had traumatic experiences, especially protracted ones, are more susceptible to anxiety. Long-term exposure to abuse or violence often severely affects an individual.

Brain chemistry has also been offered as a reason for anxiety.

This theory is promoted primarily because anxiety is quickly relieved by medications that alter the levels of certain chemicals in the brain.

Finally, personality seems to play a significant role in the development of anxiety. For example, people with low self-esteem and poor coping skills seem more susceptible to anxiety. We see that people who feel a sense of power and control over their worlds have less anxiety than those who feel a sense of inadequacy in controlling what happens to them.

Let us become more specific and look at a model for the causes of anxiety put forth by David Sheehan, M.D., who has written the popular book *The Anxiety Disease*. He proposes a model that focuses on the interplay of three forces. Let's examine them closely.

THERE IS NO QUESTION THAT THE PROBLEM OF ANXIETY IS A NODAL POINT AT WHICH THE MOST VARIOUS AND IMPORTANT QUESTIONS CONVERGE, A RIDDLE WHOSE SOLUTION WOULD BE BOUND TO THROW A FLOOD OF LIGHT ON OUR WHOLE MENTAL EXISTENCE.

—*Sigmund Freud*

**Biological.** First, Dr. Sheehan notes that biology, as stated above, plays a vital and important role in the development of an anxiety disorder. He says, "The central force in the anxiety disease appears to be a physical one. The proposed model suggests that at the center of this disease, feeding it like a spring, is a biological and probably a biochemical disorder" (Sheehan, p. 82).

Dr. Sheehan goes on to note that one of the suggestions that anxiety could be physical comes from the individuals themselves. You may identify with those that believe that it must be physical, because a psychological explanation simply does not fit your circumstances. Perhaps everything in your life is going reasonable well, and yet you still have panic symptoms at times. How can this be, you wonder? Many are at a loss to explain their anxiety in any terms other than physical problems.

Dr. Sheehan then notes the studies of genetics, as already mentioned, and explores the genetic predisposition that seems to exist. Statistical studies have shown a prevalence for the disorder within families. Close relatives are more likely to develop the disorder. The evidence suggests that there is an inheritance pattern that is passed down by one parent.

There is also evidence that the anxiety disease is associated with the presence of the heart condition known as mitral valve prolapse. He notes that in patients with panic anxiety, one in three have mitral valve prolapse.

But what is the biochemical action that is taking place that leads to anxiety? There, unfortunately, Dr. Sheehan leaves us with some questions. The answers are not conclusive, but there is much evidence pointing to a biochemical aspect to problems with anxiety. He offers the following possible explanation:

"The best guesses so far involve certain nerve endings and receptors in the central nervous system which produce and receive chemical messengers that stimulate and excite the brain. These nerve endings manufacture naturally occurring stimulants called catecholamines. It is believed that in the anxiety disease the nerve endings are overfiring. They are working too hard, overproducing these stimulants and perhaps others" (Sheehan, p. 83).

He goes on to add that at the same time there are inhibitory neurotransmitters (that calm down and dampen nerve firing) that appear to be deficient, either in quantity or quality. Certainly more research is needed, and is being done, to determine the exact nature of these interactions and their effect in the creation of anxiety.

**Conditioning.** Most of us have heard about Pavlov and his salivating dogs. Dr. Pavlov made a name for himself, and a place in history, by discovering that he could teach dogs to salivate at the ringing of a bell that had come to be associated with approaching food. Dr. Sheehan reminds us that this same operation is in effect with many who have come to develop certain anxiety disturbances.

For example, a person who experiences a physical assault while in a subway may develop anxiety symptoms the next time he or she is in a subway. Those symptoms were not there before. But after the attack, the subway becomes associated with the attack, and anxiety may persist well beyond the time and date of the attack.

Many victims of physical or emotional trauma will relate to this phenomenon. It is not unusual (and you may be experiencing this yourself) for a certain place to become associated with previous trauma. Even smells can bring flashbacks of previous trauma. For the victim of sexual molestation there may be many traumas associated with the victimization. The bedroom may be a terrifying place, or perhaps the dark has come to be associated with trauma. There may be many "triggers" that you are aware of, and some that linger in your subconscious that still have an effect upon you.

At this point I want to give a brief word about new advances in the field of trauma. My understanding is that even apparently minor traumas can create conditioning that will stimulate anxiety reactions. Something as apparently benign as being yelled at as a child by a certain parent in a certain room may later be "triggered" by someone yelling at the person after he or she has reached adulthood. The person may have developed a conditioned response—learned, and perhaps even biochemically laid-down—that leads to a certain anxiety response. Theories are emerging that suggest that the mind "remembers" biochemically, which creates lasting trauma. (Work in the field of Eye Movement Desensitization and Reprocessing appears to be promising.)

A related phenomenon to conditioning sometimes occurs, which can exacerbate the problem. The phenomenon is called *stimulus generalization,* indicating that places and events similar to the original traumatic scene can take on anxiety-provoking properties. It need not be the subway alone that causes problems, but perhaps trains and other modes of transportation. As the anxiety becomes generalized, a greater number of settings become new triggers for phobic reactions and avoidance behaviors.

Dr. Sheehan gives the illustration of a drop falling into a perfectly smooth pond. After the drop hits the surface, the ripples spread quickly out to more distant areas on the pond. The effects of the drop are felt far beyond the original point of impact. Anxiety can act in much the same way.

Another example may help to illustrate this phenomenon. Suppose a person is bitten by a dog while walking down a sidewalk. Previously they had enjoyed dogs and other animals. But after this traumatic experience the person not only avoids dogs, but any furry animal. The drop of water expands out in many directions automatically. The person avoids dogs, cats, and even furry objects.

Unfortunately, other automatic behaviors take place that add to the complexity of the situation. It is common for the person experiencing generalized anxiety to begin avoidance behaviors. That is, the person will begin to avoid anything that brings him or her into contact with any stimulus that might lead to anxiety. Unfortunately, this only adds to the intensity of the anxiety and reinforces the anxious condition. In working with the anxious person it is understood that we must help the person acknowledge avoidances that have developed and deal with them in a new way.

Let us look at another example. Imagine that a person is driving over a bridge and gets caught in an accident. The person is trapped in that traffic snarl for several hours, which leads to feelings of being trapped and mounting anxiety. The person comes to associate that experience, and bridges, with anxiety. After that terrible experience, it is natural for that person to avoid bridges, and while doing so experience the relief that comes from staying away from that uncomfortable situation. The relief of escaping from something unpleasant is very reinforcing and will lead the person to avoid similar situations more quickly the next time. This is where grandma's advice to "get back on the horse and ride it" makes some sense. But more about that later.

**Stress.** Stress is everywhere; we cannot be avoid it. If you are alive and breathing (and I trust that you are) you have some stress in your life. We are bombarded by stress every day in various forms. Let's consider a few of them:

- Hectic schedules
- Relationship challenges
- Work demands
- Family demands
- Financial challenges
- Information overload
- Health concerns
- Grief and loss issues
- Time pressures
- Performance pressures
- Crowding
- Weather

These are simply a few of the many stressors that bombard us on a daily basis. Many times we do not even consider these stressors and the impact they may be having on our lives. In fact, that is one of the problems. We do not give stress the consideration it deserves. Many, for example, continue to push themselves beyond reasonable limits because "the demands on me just keep on coming."

I am reminded of our friend Tammy and her overwhelming life experiences that led to her having a generalized anxiety disorder (GAD). Remember that her life was characterized by time pressures, performance standards and pressures, work and family demands, as well as the incessant litany of thoughts that ran through her mind causing her sleeplessness and fatigue. Her fatigue, then, only added to her inability to cope with life and enjoy the zest she formerly knew. Depression then becomes a common companion with anxiety, serving only to worsen the situation. Tammy will eventually be forced, in one way or another, to reexamine her situation.

Dr. Sheehan suggests, and this is supported by most who study anxiety, that stress is a major culprit in the anxiety disease. He notes some of the many obvious *environmental* sources of stress in our fast-paced society such as loss of a job, threatened health, or financial struggles. The stress can be more traumatic, as I have suggested, such as being the victim of a rape or robbery, or suffering the death of a loved one.

A second variety of stress is also worth considering, according to Dr. Sheehan. He mentions the anxiety that surfaces as the result of conflicts originating *within* ourselves. There may be two opposing forces within us that challenge our ability to cope. Perhaps there is a strong desire to do something, and yet the belief that to do it would be self-destructive. You may be torn about leaving a spouse, and yet doing so may violate your beliefs and convictions. These experiences can cause significant anxiety.

Dr. Sheehan suggests that environmental stress is usually not sufficient to be the cause of a severe anxiety reaction, but can be an aggravator. "It is neither necessary nor sufficient to cause the disease; but when it is present, it seems to make things worse. It may speed up the onset, intensify the symptoms, weaken the resistance and coping of the patient, accelerate the deterioration, and delay the healing" (Sheehan, p 99).

Dr. Richard Lazarus, noted authority and researcher on stress, suggests that stress begins with one's appraisal of a situation. Anxious and "stressed people" often perceive events as dangerous and believe that they do not have the resources to cope. Given this scenario we can see how someone would feel anxiety. The primitive "fight or flight" response, originally needed to escape the saber-toothed tiger but unnecessary today, creates undue anxiety. We will discuss this in more detail when we talk about treatment approaches.

While an incident of stress is usually not enough to be debilitating, chronic stress is another matter. Research is clear that chronic stress can be damaging to almost any bodily system. In addition to anxiety, chronic stress can trigger changes in the lungs that may lead to asthma, while loss of insulin during the stress response can contribute to the onset of diabetes. Evidence suggests that chronic stress can lead to muscle weakness, gastrointestinal problems, elevated blood pressure—the list of physical effects is almost endless. Of course, when the immune system is affected and we are feeling bad, we often are more susceptible to handling stress ineffectively. The vicious cycle continues.

TRUST IN THE LORD WITH ALL YOUR
HEART AND LEAN NOT TO YOUR OWN
UNDERSTANDING; IN ALL YOUR WAYS
ACKNOWLEDGE HIM AND HE WILL MAKE
YOUR PATHS STRAIGHT.

—*Proverbs 3:5-6 (NIV)*

**Spiritual Causes and Considerations.** I go beyond the three explanations offered by Dr. Sheehan and offer one more of my own—or rather, God's—to the list of contributors to the problem of anxiety. It is my opinion that just as surely as there are physical causes for our anxiety—and physical manifestations of those problems—there are also spiritual issues at hand. We are spiritual beings as well as physical ones. Let's look at some spiritual issues that may be causing distress in your life.

Imagine living life without a compass to tell you where you are going or how to get there. Imagine the feeling (anxiety) that comes from drifting through life without knowing whether what you are doing is going to get you the desired results. Many live without a compass, or roadmap, that can assure them that they are moving in the right direction. It is only after they have strayed far off the beaten path that they wake up, come to their senses, and look for a map or compass.

It seems that many live their lives this way, and I believe that it causes significant anxiety. They are like the wanderers who have lost their way and suffer the feeling of anxiety that comes from being lost. God has given us His Word to help us make decisions for daily living. The Scriptures are immensely practical, answering many of the questions that haunt us about how we should conduct our lives. Yet, so many do not pull out the manual, or roadmap, until they are helplessly lost.

The Scriptures are filled with examples of folks, like you and me, who struggle to live a pure and honorable life. Yet, again like you and me, they seem to fail time and time again. Consider David's life. You are probably familiar with the story. Here was "a man after God's own heart" who lived for years in terror and anxiety. Why? Because he was caught up in his own selfish pride and ambitions. He was the king of Israel, with all of his wants and needs met at his command. Yet he wanted more. (Sound familiar?) His lust led him to adultery, murder, and deception. Not content to live with the fabulous wealth and the position of power that God had given to him, he sought more and more. He wanted someone else's wife, which led to the murder of her husband and subsequent heartache for David.

David conspired a scheme to have the husband of the woman he desired killed in battle. When David should have been out with his army of men fighting, he was scheming to get what he wanted. He arranged for, and succeeded in, having this man killed so that he could have his wife. While his plan succeeded, it was improper, immoral, and against God's laws. David had to be confronted by the prophet Nathan before he recognized how deeply he had drifted into sin. But to his credit, he repented and turned back to God.

Listen for a moment to his cry to God after he had sinned and his conscience would not keep silent:

"Have mercy on me, O God, according to your unfailing love; according to your great compassion blot out my transgressions. Wash away all my iniquity and cleanse me from my sin. For I know my transgressions, and my sin is always before me" (Psalm 51: 1-3).

"When I kept silent, my bones wasted away through my groaning all day long. For day and night your hand was heavy upon me; my strength was sapped as in the heat of summer. Then I acknowledged my sin to you and did not cover up my iniquity" (Psalm 32: 3-5a).

David experienced what millions of others have discovered: We cannot live in violation of the laws of God without a penalty—usually involving anxiety, discouragement, and pain. We cannot live in conflict with our conscience, which hopefully has been tuned to righteous standards. When we disobey those standards, we will feel the natural accompanying anxiety and distress. Like the pain that comes from the hand touching a hot stove, this pain is good for us—it warns us of impending danger. Consider today what God may be trying to tell you by your symptoms of anxiety.

WE WAIT IN HOPE FOR THE LORD;
HE IS OUR HELP AND OUR SHIELD.

—*Psalm 33:20*

Perhaps you can relate in some way to David's story. You may have drifted from the protection of God's hand covering your life. You may have wandered from the laws of God that are set out so you can enjoy life without anxiety. Out from under that protection, you may have decided to listen to your own "wisdom," which tends to be tainted by worldly standards. This has left you vulnerable to your own deceptive thinking and natural desires, culminating in sin and pain.

Listen to a final encouraging word from David to us: "Why are you downcast, O my soul? Why so disturbed within me? Put your hope in God, for I will yet praise him, my Savior and my God." (Psalm 43:5)

# TREATMENT CONSIDERATIONS

If you are troubled with anxiety, you have probably seen yourself in one or more of the different disorders that have been mentioned. It is my hope that at this point you are not feeling alone, but that instead you have a sense of expectation that you will find some answers to the problems you are facing. While this **Pocket Therapist** is not meant to be exhaustive, it will give you many answers and point you in the right direction for other help that you will need.

Although every person's condition is unique, most anxiety disorders are going to fall within the categories that have already been mentioned. Furthermore, *anxiety is a very treatable condition.* You do not need to suffer any longer.

Your **first** task is to face the fact that *you must become active in combating your particular problem*. No one will care as much about your well-being as you! This is a critical concept and one that I hope you will rehearse and internalize. You must be active in understanding your particular problem and the treatment approaches that have been found to be effective. There are many treatment approaches that are outdated, ineffective, and useless for your particular problem. Learn all you can about your condition.

This leads me to your **second** task. *You must find a team of professionals who have training in the field of anxiety disorders.* A generalist is less likely to be aware of current research and treatment options for these debilitating, and very frustrating, conditions. Ask around and find a psychologist and physician who understand anxiety and effective treatment approaches. Don't be afraid to interview your clinician on the phone to verify his or her understanding of these disorders.

Continuing on in this vein, if the physicians or therapists you have been working with are giving you unhelpful platitudes, fire them. If you have been on a tranquilizer for years without significant benefit, ask some pointed questions. If the psychologist you have seen is not helping you get your desired results, seek another opinion. Your must find the right team of clinicians *whom you trust to take you to the next level in your recovery.* But, you must be honest with yourself and make sure that you are following their prescriptions and recommendations. You must also be honest with them regarding your frustration.

Having hand selected the right team, we are ready to talk about specific interventions. There are many, so get ready to feel slightly overwhelmed. The fact that there are many useful tools is a positive thing, however. We would rather have many useful tools than just one in our tool bag.

Generally speaking, most anxiety disorders respond to a two-pronged treatment approach: *medication and psychotherapy.* Let's begin our discussion with the topic of medications. I must admit, from the outset, that I am not a physician and am not an expert in this field. That is why you must find someone, possibly a psychiatrist who specializes in the treatment of anxiety disorders, to help you find the right medication for your condition. Many general practitioners and internal medicine physicians will be able to help you with this problem, but some will be more comfortable referring you to a specialist.

Having found the right clinician for your particular problem, let's look specifically at the treatment interventions.

# MEDICATIONS

When people think of medications for the treatment of anxiety they, unfortunately, seem to first think of "street drugs." They wonder, "Will I get hooked on them? Will they make me feel like a zombie? Will I become some other person?" It is not that these questions are totally impossible, but rather that with proper management these possibilities are extremely improbable.

Perhaps the most important point to emphasize from the onset of this discussion is that these medications can work wonders in the treatment of anxiety disorders, but they must be managed properly. Your treating therapist must work closely with your physician to ensure that you are getting the best of both worlds. Both worlds, again, involve the worlds of medication and psychotherapy. These are the primary tools that you will be using in managing, treating, and recovery from anxiety.

Because I am not a physician, please forgive me for being very careful about making blanket statements regarding medications. I will be using some generalities because this is an area to be discussed thoroughly with your physician. Your therapist, incidentally, should not be making specific recommendations about medications unless he or she has had the requisite training to do so. Inquire specifically about this if your therapist begins to violate those boundaries and act like he or she has had medical training.

Now, back to the topic of medications. Fortunately great advances have been made in the past twenty years that can help you immensely when it comes to temporary symptom management of anxiety. What follows is a discussion of what particular drugs are *generally* used for which conditions. *Remember that there are many varieties of anxiety disorders and all are not treated the same.*

**Benzodiazepines.** One of the primary groups of medications used with anxiety disorders are the benzodiazepines. These have been found to be very effective in treating generalized anxiety disorder as well as panic anxiety. They tend to be fast-acting and are often used for individuals in acute distress. Their strength is their fast-acting nature, quick relief, and general potency. The drawback with them is their potential for dependency. They can also have the side effect of drowsiness and an experiencing of the anxiety symptoms when the drug is discontinued. Because of the dependency potential, some may experience withdrawal symptoms. However, it must be emphasized that these problems can be managed if the individual and doctor work closely with one another.

**Tricyclics (TCAs).** The tricyclics have been around for some time; however, there are newer ones that seem to have increased effectiveness. While these drugs were first used for the treatment of depression, and still are, some are also quite effective in the treatment of anxiety disorders. Many tricyclics are used in the treatment of PTSD and some are used in treating OCD. As with most medications, selection and management of the most appropriate medication for the condition is a precarious matter. You will need to be well informed about side effects, which often include weight gain, dry mouth, and, at times, impaired sexual function. Again, remember that by managing the dosage most side effects are manageable.

**Selective Serotonin Reuptake Inhibitor (SSRIs).** These are the newest medications available in the treatment of depression and anxiety, and they appear to have brought treatment to a higher level. There are several SSRIs used for anxiety disorders, and they are also often used for OCD. There seem to be relatively few difficult side effects and these tend to disappear over time.

**Beta Blockers.** These drugs have also been used in the management and treatment of anxiety disorders. They have been used especially for symptoms like palpitations, sweating, and tremors. They have commonly been used for those suffering from the anxiety associated with social phobia. They tend to reduce blood flow and slow the heartbeat.

**MonoAmine Oxidase Inhibitors (MAOs).** While MAOs have been around for quite a while, they tend not to be a first-line approach in the treatment of anxiety disorders. They do, however, have their place in the arsenal of treatment tools. They have been used in the treatment of panic anxiety, social phobia, PTSD, and sometimes OCD. The primary drawback involves dietary restriction necessary when using these drugs. Anyone taking an MAO must avoid certain medications, alcoholic beverages, and foods such as cheese that contain tyramine.

# PSYCHOTHERAPY

Having considered medications and the role they may play in the treatment of anxiety, let's now look at the primary psychotherapy treatment tools at our disposal. Fortunately, there are many tools available. I recommend that you familiarize yourself with all of these methods and choose the ones that work best for you. Some will sound intriguing, but may not be of much use to you. Find the ones that not only work for you, but that you will continue to use. Be honest with yourself and your level of motivation. Hopefully, because you are in distress and want relief, you will be motivated to do the research and make the proper selection of tools for your situation.

One more comment about psychotherapy is in order. We tend to be rather lazy when it comes to wanting our distressing symptoms to disappear. Why not take a pill rather than do the work involved in therapy? There are several answers to this question.

First, studies have clearly shown that medications for the treatment of anxiety are enhanced by therapy. One without the other is not as effective as both combined.

Second, while it may be easier to take a pill, that does not necessarily reach the problems that need to be addressed. For example, if you are working at a stressful job, there are pills that will take away the anxiety but not deal with the personality traits that keep you attached to that job, or your need to work as hard as you do. If you do not work on the problematic personality traits, your symptoms will return the moment you quit taking the medications.

A third issue is the importance of becoming acquainted with our bodies, listening to them for clues about what needs to change. Anxiety can be a good thing in warning us of some danger or imbalance in our lives. Distress can be a powerful motivator in getting us to change a troubling situation. Emotional pain is a mighty motivator to get us on our knees to ask for help.

Now, having set the stage for understanding the benefits of psychotherapy, let's look at some of the common models and tools that are available to you. Remember that this list is growing every day and there is no way that I can include all of the possible tools in this booklet. Get out and look for yourselves at what is available to lower your anxiety and increase your feelings of general well-being.

There are two primary models of treatment for anxiety when it comes to nonmedical therapy. They are cognitive and behavior therapy. Actually, the two are often combined to form a model of treatment called Cognitive-Behavior Therapy. Let's take a look at these models of treatment.

**Cognitive Therapy.** Cognitive therapy has the advantage of being the most heavily researched form of psychotherapy. It has subsequently been proven effective in the treatment of many emotional problems, including the anxiety disorders. Because of its effectiveness, it needs to be in your arsenal of tools.

Cognitive therapy is based upon a relatively simple notion. The way we react to situations is based upon our view of the world and what we tell ourselves about those events. It has been found that people with anxiety disorders (and depression, for that matter) tend to process information and evaluate their circumstances differently than nonanxious folks. Anxious and depressed people tend to have many "thinking errors" or cognitive distortions that, once corrected, help in alleviating difficult emotions.

There are several key theorists who have developed models for working with cognitions as a remedy for our anxiety. If you want to read further on this topic see the appendix for names of additional books on the topic. For the most part their theories and treatment tools are similar. One simple model I have learned and practiced involves the ABCs.

A= The *activating* event (A friend being late for your dinner party)

B= The *belief* you hold about that event ("One should never be late")

C= The *consequent* emotion (Anger)

The interesting thing about this model is that you can change how you think about an event, and subsequently can change your emotions. For example, if you *decide* that it is okay for someone to be late, you will probably not be annoyed. Better yet, if you decide that you can use the time to relax while you wait for them, you can be restful and at peace. *You decide, then, how you are going to feel.*

When we look closely at how anxious people view the world, we hear a lot of *catastrophizing*. They see something as "terrible" when it is simply "unfortunate." Anxious people tend to see the world in terms of black and white, and think things have to turn out a certain way. They try to control things that they have no control over. When things go wrong, as they invariably do, they tend to believe it is the end of the world.

**Try this:** Take a moment and think of a situation that is troubling you currently. What is the activating event, or current circumstance that is troubling you? What is your belief about that situation? What is your emotion as a consequence of the belief that you have? Finally, how could you change your view of that situation so that you would feel better?

THE THING THAT UPSETS PEOPLE THE
MOST IS NOT WHAT HAPPENS, BUT WHAT
THEY THINK IT MEANS.

*—Epictetus*

*Thinking*

Cognitive therapy has found that people make all kinds of erro-
neous assumptions about things. We tend to think the worst
about a situation. We make arbitrary assumptions about what
is happening, and we are often wrong. Often these have become
habitual ways of viewing the world, and we need a therapist to
point them out to us. Challenging and changing our negative
thoughts is one of the primary concerns of cognitive therapy.

Albert Ellis was one of the pioneers of cognitive therapy and helped us to look at our *irrational beliefs* that feed our anxiety. Consider some of the following irrational beliefs, and perhaps you will see yourself in some of them.

- I must be liked by everyone
- Everything must go as I have planned it
- People should always be kind to me
- I should never feel or be rejected
- I should do everything perfectly
- I must do my best

Of course there are many other "shoulds" we could add to the above list. You might want to take a few minutes and consider what irrational thoughts you have that feed your anxiety and lower your self-esteem. The next time you feel upset you might want to take a look at your beliefs and consider how you can change them.

Another aspect of cognitive therapy has to do with *focus*. Cognitive therapists argue that we need not focus our attention on all of the things that are going wrong, but focus instead on what is going right, and what we can do to effectively alter our situation. This has certainly proven to be a valuable tool for many.

Dr. Chris Thurman has developed a model of cognitive therapy incorporating biblical principles that is worth considering. He believes, as do most cognitive therapists, that our beliefs about the world, the future, and ourselves impact our emotions and behavior. He believes that the *truth* will set us free.

T= Trigger event—where life events and situations happen to us

R= Wrong thinking—thoughts about the event that are faulty

U= Unhealthy response—emotional and behavioral reactions that are unhelpful

T= Truth—determining the truth about the situation

H= Healthy response—emotional and behavioral reactions that are healthy

Dr. Thurman would suggest that our unhealthy responses occur because of faulty thinking, and we are the ones who can change and control this aspect of our lives. It is a powerful tool that is available to you. You can reconsider problematic situations; you can reason things out; you can see what the Bible has to say about a situation.

**Behavior Therapy.** Behavior therapy is the other prong of a two-pronged electrical plug that can save your life. Change how you act, and you can change how you feel. It might sound too simple, but it is true. Just as surely as we need to change our minds, we must also learn to change how we act. Another common way to phrase this concept is "fake it until you make it."

But what exactly is behavior therapy? The answer is complicated because it includes many different tools. I will list several, but again I encourage you to do some more research to find other tools that may work for you.

**Exposure Therapy.** In exposure therapy the person is exposed to the feared situation until he or she has become desensitized to it. For example, if you were afraid of elevators, you would ride in them time and time again, perhaps after learning the art of relaxation therapy, until they are no longer fearful to you. Or perhaps you would gradually spend more time in social situations until they were no longer fearful to you. Remember that to avoid a situation usually leads to being fearful of that situation indefinitely.

Exposure therapy is particularly effective in the treatment of phobias and with OCD. When used in the treatment of depression we would arrange a set of behaviors that would reduce a person's isolation and create positive experiences to reinforce self-esteem and empowerment over their lives. This can also be helpful for those struggling with anxiety.

**Relaxation training.** Relaxation Training is another form of behavior therapy. Relaxation training is helpful because it alters the muscular tension that results from anxiety. Relaxation also aids in the learning of new skills, which will help anxiety and depression.

Relaxation training involves becoming aware of the physical sensations of muscular tension and relaxation. People can become quite adept at recognizing physical cues that tell them that they are becoming anxious. Consequently, they can develop techniques to help them alleviate that tension and anxiety.

In 1929 Edmund Jacobson, a Chicago physician, in his book *Progressive Relaxation* presented a theory that still holds true today. He suggested that if we learn to relax in response to stressful situations we can replace previously learned anxiety responses. Today you can learn progressive relaxation in a relatively short time. It involves mentally scanning the body, starting from head to toe, and releasing any tension that is felt there.

**Try this:** Here is a very brief progressive relaxation exercise. Sit in a very comfortable position. Begin with your hands, forearms, and biceps. Concentrate on that area of the body and let the tension dissolve. It may be helpful to use the words "Let go of the tension."

Now move to the head, face, throat, and shoulders. Focus on each area and practice letting go of the tension in each of these areas. You can practice tensing them before letting go of the tension, keeping your eyes closed.

Now move to your chest, stomach, and lower back. Let go of the tension in these areas. Tell yourself that you are feeling calm and rested. Tense each area and then let go of the tension.

Finally, move to your thighs, buttocks, calves, and feet. Tense these areas and then, as you let go, tell yourself that you are feeling calm and rested.

Practice this two times per day for fifteen minutes each time. You will be surprised at the results if you practice this faithfully.

Learning the art of *deep breathing* has been found to enhance relaxation training. It has been found that proper breathing is an antidote to stress. It has also been found that few of us breathe in the proper way. You may be thinking, as I have, that there cannot be an improper way to breathe. I no longer believe that statement.

Without fully explaining the rationale for proper breathing, which would take some doing, suffice it to say that proper breathing, and deep breathing, can be a powerful tool to aid you in decreasing your anxiety.

**Try this:** Lie down on a blanket on the floor. Bend your knees so that your feet are about eight inches apart. Make sure that your spine is straight as you scan your body for tension. Practice letting go of the tension as you begin to practice deep breathing. Place one hand on your abdomen and the other on your chest. Inhale slowly and deeply through your nose into your abdomen to push up your hand. Your chest should hardly move as you practice taking air into your abdomen.

Next practice inhaling through your nose and exhaling through your mouth. Take long, slow, deep breaths and feel your abdomen rising in the process. Practice this form of deep breathing for five or ten minutes at a time. You can practice it more often when you are feeling tense.

**Meditation.** There has been much controversy about meditation. The controversy, however, stems not in the act but in the *object* of our meditation. For our purposes I recommend that you meditate upon a favorite Scripture. The psalmist said, "I meditate upon your precepts and consider your ways" (Psalm 119:15, NIV).

Consider practicing progressive relaxation and deep breathing when focusing upon a favorite Scripture. Let the words of the Scripture melt into your being, bringing a sense of peacefulness.

There are many other methods and tools in dealing with anxiety that are available to you that cannot be listed in this **Pocket Therapist.** You will find some helpful and others not so helpful. You may also find that some are questionable in light of your faith beliefs. You must use some discretion and caution when looking into tools advertised for the elimination of anxiety. You may also be well served to remember to "chew up the meat, and spit out the bones." In other words, take what is useful and discard the rest. For a comprehensive discussion of tools available to assist in ridding you of anxiety, I refer you to a popular workbook, *The Relaxation & Stress Reduction Workbook,* cited in the appendix.

# Summary

Anxiety is one of the most distressing feelings in the world. It seems that we live in an age of anxiety. But *we have a choice.* We are not destined to feel anxious. While we may be under a lot of stress, or somehow have received a constitution prone to anxiety, there are a multitude of tools that we can explore that will greatly reduce or eliminate anxiety. There are also new and improved medications that will be immensely helpful as well. Find the combination of tools that works best for you.

God bless as you journey into healing and wholeness.

# RECOMMENDED READING

1. Beck, A.T.; Emory, G.D.; & Greenberg, R.L. *Anxiety Disorders and Phobias: A Cognitive Perspective.* New York: Basic Books, 1985.

2. Beck, A.T.; Rush, A.J.; Shaw, B. F.; & Emory, G.D. *Cognitive Therapy of Depression.* New York: Guilford Press, 1979.

3. Burns, David. *Feeling Good.* New York: William Morrow, 1980.

4. Sheehan, David. *The Anxiety Disease.* New York: Bantam Books, 1985.

5. Davis, Martha; Eshelman, Elizabeth Robbins; & McKay, Matthew. *The Relaxation & Stress Reduction Workbook.* Oakland: New Harbinger Publications, 1990.

6. Handly, Robert and Neff, Pauline. *Anxiety and Panic Attacks.* New York: Ballantine Books, 1985.